"Send me butterflies"

By
KIMBERLY DENISE WADE

"Send me butterflies"
Copyright © 2016 Kimberly Denise Wade

All rights reserved. No part of this book may be reproduced (except for inclusion in reviews), disseminated or utilized in any form or by any means, electronic or mechanical, including photocopying, recording, or in any information storage and retrieval system, or the Internet/World Wide Web without written permission from the author or publisher.

Printed in the United States of America
First Edition Printing

Design by
Arbor Services, Inc.
http://www.arborservices.co/

ISBN: 978-0-692-76493-0
LCCN: 2016913663

1. Title 2. Author 3. Memoir

Dedication

To my God, who gave me a new perspective on life and thousands of blessings during this trial.

———————

To my wonderful husband, Jon, who is my rock for which I can rest on.

———————

To my amazing son, Jacky, who keeps me smiling.

———————

To my mini me, Angel Jonny, whom I miss every single second of my life.

Contents

Forward 1

Chapter 1 - The Day Jonny Went Away 3

Chapter 2 - The Diagnosis 11

Chapter 3 - Surgery Day 17

Chapter 4 - All about the Posts 25

Chapter 5 - Jumped the Gun 33

Chapter 6 - All the Support 37

Chapter 7 - God Appears 43

Chapter 8 - A Piece at a Time 55

Chapter 9 - Twin Brothers 63

Chapter 10 - Mr. Wonderful 69

Chapter 11 - A Blessing of Memory Loss 73

Chapter 12 - Acceptance 79

Chapter 13 - Two Balloons for Heaven 85

Chapter 14 - State of the Union 93

Chapter 15 - Having Faith 99

About the Author 105

Forward

The journey of our lives is full of twists and turns. We never really know what is around the next bend. This story is the reflection of a mother who was totally unprepared for what she found on the path in front of her and her twin son. This is the story of love and loss, and finally a realization of a bigger purpose.

Sometimes the thing you lose can be so great, you actually lose yourself instead of the possession. When all we knew and loved before was destroyed…it didn't feel like we suffered a loss; we BECAME lost. This story is a story of our transition from lost to found. While we were being hollowed out with sadness, we were being filled with something else. This fiery furnace that was destroying our lives, was actually burning away impurities and leaving us better in the end with a pure faith and dependence on God. We found in our frailty and weakness that we have an unbreakable strength that does not come from us. We saw through our submission to this disease that we were really finally free; free to let go of our

Kimberly Denise Wade

plans and follow the life that God intends. We learned that miracles happen every day if you open your eyes and see them.

We have a choice in how we see the world. You can see us as just another cancer statistic. Or you can see us like I do; my wife a survivor and my son a hero. That is how I see it, and it makes all the difference for me. I hope that by reading this book, you will learn to control your perspective and face your giants head on with the full knowledge that you will overcome. Blessings to you and yours.

— Jon Wade

Chapter 1
The Day Jonny Went Away

Everything I describe in this book was part of God's plan. A lot of people talk about "following God's plan," when what they mean is getting God's help in carrying out their own plans, their own agenda. We all do it. Praying we get that job, we get a winning lottery ticket, our favorite team wins a game, that our car starts on a cold day. We pray for so many great and small things, usually with the belief that God isn't a guiding force, but rather some sort of genie who will grant our wishes if we just believe in Him.

But I should say something about my plan first. I live in Jerseyville, Illinois, a town northeast of St. Louis about thirty minutes. I was a stay-at-home mother for fraternal twin boys, Jonny and Jacky. My older daughter was in the army and serving her country like my husband had done for many years prior. My husband, Jon, was a chief executive officer at the local hospital, and we had been married for ten years. We lived in a two-story house with two dogs, Maggie and Lucy, and we drove late-model cars. We went on vacations twice a year—one long one with the twins and a week with just Jon and me. While we attended church regularly, we weren't what anyone would describe as overly religious, but definitely spiritual. And my plan was for all of that to continue. My prayers were usually some variation on simply, "God, please just keep my life the way it is." But all in all, we were your all-American family minus the white picket fence.

It probably sounds cliché to say that Jonny was full of life, but he always made a strong impression wherever he went. At seven years old, he was high spirited, social to a fault—always introducing himself to strangers—and witty. On his first day in kindergarten, Jonny walked into the classroom and announced, "I'm here! The party can start now!" Jonny always loved school and was always popular. He was a people lover and a social butterfly. He not only took after me, but he looked like me and I would usually call him my "mini me."

Jonny was a lover of many things. Whether it was shark facts, playing baseball and basketball, decorating cookies with me, fishing with his dad, or simply talking on the phone to family, he did it with every ounce of his heart. Jonny was a sensitive soul, and many would say beyond his years.

Jonny also had an interest in God from an early age. I can remember him carrying on conversations with God as early as three years old. He would say things like, "I can't wait to see

"Send me butterflies"

God's face" or, "I can't wait for my family to be in heaven." It's the sort of thing that most parents would think was cute, talking with God as if He were just another person in our lives. But Jonny did it often and was already building the most important relationship in his life while I was still more worried about balancing housecleaning, grocery shopping, and picking up the boys from school. It's amazing how often children are able to prioritize better than adults. And that was Jonny, always showing what was most important.

When he was seven years old in early November, Jonny suggested that we celebrate Christmas by releasing a balloon for Jesus, a birthday present that would float to heaven, even before opening our gifts on Christmas morning. Jon and I thought it was a sweet idea and planned to make a little ceremony out of it. That was our plan.

Eight days before Christmas, Jonny came home from school complaining about a headache. I gave him some Tylenol and told him to get some rest. I can't say that I was too concerned about it, but still thought it was odd. When Jon got home from work, he placed his briefcase in the bar chair like he did every day, and I told him about Jonny. I'll never forget the look on his face. It seemed as if the blood had drawn out of his face and he became as white as a ghost. He said, "I hope he doesn't have a brain tumor." I remember getting angry with him for even suggesting such a horrible thing. It was just a headache after all.

Looking back, I can see that because Jon spent his days working at a hospital, he had seen too many serious conditions begin with such simple symptoms. How many times must he have seen parents bring their children in, looking for good news and reassurance, only to be told that the worst thing they could imagine had happened? How many times had he quietly made the same prayer that I had made to God? Please keep everything just the way it is. Please don't let that happen to me and mine.

The next few days were the usual flurry of activity that most families experience right before Christmas—last-minute gift shopping, planning various get-togethers, baking cookies, and keeping track of the children now that school had let out for winter break. This year, I had a new tradition planned of Christmas Eve boxes for each of the boys and Jon. They were filled with hot chocolate, homemade cookies, their favorite candy, a special Christmas mug, a pair of matching pajamas, and of course, their favorite movie to be watched on Christmas Eve all together as a family. It was going to be a spectacular event, and the boys were excited about the new tradition along with our annual matching pajama picture in front of our beautifully decorated Christmas tree. But during

"Send me butterflies"

all of that, I noticed that Jonny's headaches were coming with an increased frequency. Jon's fear of a brain tumor stayed in the back of my mind, but I kept telling myself that it was a ridiculous conclusion. After all, I'd been suffering from migraine headaches for years, as had a number of family members; Jonny was probably just dealing with the same thing.

On December 22, the Monday before Christmas, Jonny woke up crying, saying the headaches were getting worse. Any thoughts I had about Tylenol being able to fix my son's headache vanished when he began to throw up. I contacted our pediatrician immediately but couldn't get an appointment until the following day. Now I was worried. Very worried.

On Tuesday, the pediatrician put Jonny through a variety of simple tests. He checked his eyes, observed how he walked, and asked Jonny to follow the movement of his finger. Jonny easily completed all the tests, which shouldn't have surprised us in the slightest. Jonny was always coordinated. Years before, when we were teaching Jonny how to ride his bike, he hopped on his bike and took off without needing any assistance from either one of us. We were amazed and couldn't believe that we didn't need to help hold him up like most parents did with their children. I mean, Jonny was only five years old at the time. I remember as we walked down the street that day, watching him ride for the first time, he looked at me and said,

"Look, Mom, no feet!" as his feet stuck straight out side to side. Yes, he had amazing coordination and balance, so for him to pass these tests was not a surprise to either one of us.

When the doctor asked about other symptoms, I told him there were none. After the tests were finished, and because the headaches and vomiting were the only symptoms, the pediatrician was inclined to agree with me that it was probably just a migraine. However, Jon's concern about a possible brain tumor still nagged at me, and I shared it with the doctor. He agreed to schedule an MRI and stated that it was more to set my mind at ease than out of any real belief that Jonny might have a brain tumor. Unfortunately, he wasn't able to schedule the MRI until the day after Christmas, which would mean a few more days of worry for both Jon and me.

For the next two days, I continued giving Jonny Tylenol and focused on the December 26 MRI. Of course, what I was hoping was that the MRI would find nothing wrong, which wouldn't help to alleviate Jonny's headaches but would settle my own growing fear that this was something worse than a migraine. But on Christmas morning, just after five a.m., Jonny began screaming with pain. All of our plans to open presents, meet with family, and send off a birthday balloon for Jesus were gone. We drove Jonny to the closest children's

"Send me butterflies"

hospital immediately, which was forty-five minutes away, since we were unable to wait one more day for the scheduled MRI. But by the time we reached the hospital, Jonny had begun to feel better. At the time, we thought perhaps the headache was a passing ailment after all, and the emergency room doctor didn't seem overly concerned about it. However, what we later learned was that the intensity of the headache depended on Jonny's physical position. When he was sitting up, the pain grew worse, while it eased up whenever he was lying flat. So during the trip to the hospital, when he was lying flat in the car, the pain had eased up. Not realizing that the problem hadn't gotten better, the doctor sent us back home to enjoy our Christmas afternoon. When we realized Jonny felt better lying flat, we kept him lying down and had a good time even though he wasn't feeling well. We didn't even open all of our presents, as Jonny couldn't fully enjoy the day.

The following morning, the day after Christmas, began with Jonny screaming again about the pain. He'd begun hitting himself in the head and even pulling out his hair in clumps. At that point, it was obvious that Jonny was dealing with something worse than a migraine headache. I got down on my hands and knees and prayed over and over again, as I was utterly terrified.

That morning, my husband and I and both boys returned to the hospital early in the morning so Jonny could finally get the MRI that we hoped would tell us we had nothing to worry about. But Jon and I both knew at that point that something was seriously wrong, although we still hoped it wasn't a brain tumor. That surely couldn't happen to Jonny.

December 26, 2014, would be the day that we were reminded that God's plan is not necessarily the same as ours. I will never forget that Jacky, Jonny's seven-year-old twin, called it the day Jonny went away.

Chapter 2
The Diagnosis

Most people don't even know what MRI stands for: magnetic resonance imaging. They know that it's a special type of camera that takes pictures of what's inside a person's body, tissue rather than bones like that of an X-ray. An MRI machine looks like a giant tube big enough for a human body to slide through. But most people don't know what they sound like. They might assume that these high-tech devices give off a low hum like a microwave oven. I'd had several MRI scans done on myself in the past, so I was prepared for the noise, but there's no way Jonny was ready for it, and I worried for him.

Imagine a seven-year-old boy, feeling something worse than the worst headache he's ever had. Now imagine placing him on a bed and telling him to remain absolutely still while he's fed into a giant camera. The inside of that camera is dark, and when he looks at his mother for reassurance, all he can see is that she's scared, very scared. He can see out through a little mirror placed above his head, so he can keep watching his mother as the bed slides inside the camera, and at that point maybe it doesn't seem so bad. It's just a dark room, really, and he can see out of it. But then the camera starts running and all he hears are what sounds like jackhammers, sirens, and buzzing. All the while he has to remain perfectly still so the camera can get a clear picture. And he has to do that for twenty long minutes.

When was the last time you saw a seven-year-old remain perfectly still for twenty minutes? When was the last time you saw an adult remain perfectly still for twenty minutes? But Jonny did it, even through the pain and the fear.

I stood beside that machine, holding Jonny's hand during the entire process while I watched tears roll down his little cheeks. Occasionally I'd look away to check on the technician, who was standing behind a glass wall and checking the images, looking for something I hoped she'd never find. At first she was alone in that room, but then she was joined by Jon, Jacky, and another man wearing a flowered shirt. I was surprised to see them, as they were going to wait for the test to be over before they returned to the room. Even without the glass wall, I doubt I could have heard what they were saying, due to all the noise of the MRI scanner.

When the scan was finally finished, I helped Jonny off the bed and carried him to the other room to find out what they'd found, still clinging to hope that it was nothing. I was

"Send me butterflies"

told that the man who'd walked in with Jon and Jacky was a radiologist. They'd found a tumor in our son's brain and wanted to run a second MRI scan, a contrast scan he called it. I'm not sure if he explained why a second MRI was necessary. I honestly don't know if he said anything after that because I was screaming. I remember falling to my knees and knew I was going to be sick.

The radiologist escorted me out of the room into a lounge area. I couldn't focus or say anything beyond no! over and over again. Of course, I felt fear and grief, but also confusion. Not only did I not know what we were going to do next, how we were going to make this problem go away, but I couldn't figure out how this thing had happened. It hadn't been a part of my plan, after all. Jonny was supposed to scrape his knees and elbows while he was out playing. He would have the occasional broken bone, high fever, or minor accident, and that was supposed to be the level of tragedy that came into our lives while he was growing up. Someday, decades from now, Jonny was supposed to be the one talking to a doctor about my test results. Cancer was something that took parents from their children, not the other way around. That was the way these things were supposed to go.

And then I wondered if I'd done something wrong. Should I have fed Jonny organic food, without growth hormones or other chemicals? I recalled a time, two years earlier, when he'd complained about feeling something inside his ear, but it had soon gone away. Should I have taken him to a doctor back then? Would they have caught the tumor early if I had? Was this my fault? And if it was, what could I have done to fix it? I had always been able to make things better in the past.

Eventually I regained my composure, cleaned myself up from getting sick, and was led back into the screening room. The contrast MRI was already finished. I knew this was bad news but still wasn't sure how bad, so I asked, "When will we know if it's cancer?" The radiologist turned around and immediately responded, "It's cancer." I stood looking at him with my eyes wide open and filled with tears. I found it hard to process the words he had said. Surely he was wrong. He had to be wrong.

The radiologist explained that Jonny had medulloblastoma, a malignant brain tumor that resided at the base of the back of his head. He needed to have an operation immediately to remove it, as it was causing fluid to build up in his brain, resulting in high pressure. Jon immediately made arrangements with the St. Louis Children's Hospital for our son's surgery, the same hospital we'd visited the previous day, when we'd been reassured that Jonny's headaches were nothing serious and were sent home.

"Send me butterflies"

As we drove to the children's hospital, I prayed. At that point, I wasn't even asking God to help our son or make the whole thing a big misunderstanding. I simply kept asking God why it had happened at all. I mean, we were good people, so why us? None of this had been a part of my plan, so how could it have been a part of God's?

Once we arrived, the neurologist asked if I wanted to know about the risks involved with surgery, but I didn't see any point since he'd said that Jonny would die without it. I had no wish to put myself through more agony than I was already in. As the doctor spoke to me about Jonny's brain surgery, I could hear Jonny's screams in the room from the headache. I got physically sick once again. Everything was happening so quickly, and I had no control over any of it.

Chapter 3
Surgery Day

Shortly after we arrived at the children's hospital, Jon's parents arrived and took Jacky back to our house while we waited for Jonny to exit surgery. Everything was happening so quickly that Jon and I couldn't keep up with it all. I could hardly imagine how seven-year-old Jacky could manage. Many children don't even have a clear understanding of death at that age. Of course, Jacky understood what death meant on a physical level, but he had no emotional connection to the term yet. Jacky and his brother did everything together, and now he'd been told that Jonny had something serious in his brain that would change our family forever. We couldn't spare him from that idea at the time, but we could at least spare him from the miserable hospital waiting room.

I remember that the waiting room was cold. Maybe it wasn't adequately heated for that time of year, or maybe the hospital management liked to keep it cold. It was also lonely and eerily quiet. I suppose some of the staff members were enjoying extended Christmas breaks, and most families wouldn't choose to schedule a hospital appointment during a time when relatives were visiting from out of town, so only people who had no choice were there. We were emotionally and physically drained. We prayed for strength to get us through as we sat staring at each other with no words for one another. Then someone knocked on the waiting room door. Members from our church, whom we didn't even know well, had shown up. One after another came to comfort us, and we truly appreciated their presence. We soon came to realize that during this time, God was showing us love through each and every person who came through the door—an everlasting love.

This moment was a major milestone in the journey we would come to know. This is when we first saw God step in and help us when we couldn't have made it on our own. At this point our faith journey began to take shape. It would take us to a deeper faith, a deeper understanding, and a deeper purpose than we had ever known before.

Finally, right before midnight, the neurosurgeon came in to tell us that the operation had been a success for the most part, but he was careful about being too optimistic. The tumor was cancerous, and they had to leave a tiny piece, as it was attached to a large blood vessel. If they were to remove the entire tumor, Jonny would have had a massive stroke on the table. But hopefully the radiation would destroy it. Hopefully.

"Send me butterflies"

On Monday, with little sleep since Jonny had been in ICU for several days, we met with the oncologist. She stated that they had taken some fluid from his spine to test to ensure that no cancerous cells resided there. She assured us it would come back negative—only 10% ever came back positive—and went on to explain the treatment plan. I was still in shock. I was still confused. She explained it all as if she were telling me where to find milk at the grocery store. She seemed so matter of fact, but I was still reeling from this new, ugly world I had been thrust into overnight. Little did we know that, a couple days later, we would find out that cancerous cells had been found in his spinal fluid, making his survival rate even lower. Yes, he was in the 10%.

The oncologist said that once the treatment of radiation and chemotherapy killed the cancer cells, Jonny would be considered NED, a shorthand medical term meaning "no evidence of disease." And while that would seem to be spectacular news, she let us know that NED was not the same thing as being cancer free. NED simply meant no sign of cancer cells, not that none were there. If this news was not enough, Jonny would need to be tested every year for the rest of his life, and in fact, he had a 50% chance of the cancer returning within a two-year period. She went on to say that, if the cancer did return, it would be considered incurable. I felt faintish and walked out of the room, leaving Jon and the oncologist there. I couldn't breathe or comprehend what she was saying. How could the world be so advanced in technology and land a man on the moon, yet we had so few options in saving our son's life? How could she be talking about my son hand in hand with these terms? This plan didn't match mine!

Her recommendation was that Jonny immediately begin a cycle of thirty high-dose radiation treatment sessions focused on his brain and spine. Following those sessions, she further recommended six months of strong chemotherapy. Like the surgery itself, we immediately agreed to her recommendations. If it would make our son healthy again, Jon and I were prepared to agree to any treatment.

A week earlier, I'd been giving my son Tylenol to help him deal with a recurring headache. I'd been worried that Jonny might have to deal with a lifetime of migraine headaches. Now I was being told that his chances of survival were the same as a coin toss. Not only that, but the damage done to his body by both the radiation treatment and chemotherapy would carry on through the rest of his life, even if it did destroy the cancer cells completely. Not only did Jonny risk dying from this cancer, but even if he survived, he would never have his old life back. Neither Jonny nor our family would ever get "back to our normal." This was hard for me to understand or even comprehend.

"Send me butterflies"

Over the next few months, I would frequently wake up and think that Jonny's cancer had simply been a terrible nightmare. The headache had gone away and we'd celebrated Christmas the way we'd planned. But then I'd look around and see the hospital overnight bag on my bedside that I always kept nearby. I'd look at the pink bucket beside Jonny's bed that was there for when he had to throw up and couldn't make it to the bathroom, which happened almost daily, if not several times a day. The vomiting was so traumatic and left both Jon and me feeling helpless. Watching your child become so frail and continue to throw up every day was horrific, to say the least. And again, we could do nothing to help him. Nothing.

Jonny began to suffer again from severe headaches once the tumor was removed. We were at a loss, thinking that we had corrected the headache issue by removing the tumor that was blocking the fluid from draining. However, we learned that his ventricles would no longer contract, flushing the fluid from his brain. The only answer was to have a shunt placed in his brain. This mechanical piece would flush the fluid once the reservoir reached a certain point. The doctors tried a type of shunt that was automatic and the most common; it worked for 90% of children who needed shunts. Four days later, Jonny was rushed into the emergency room with severe headaches again. They replaced that shunt, yes, yet another brain surgery, and said it must have malfunctioned. Less than forty-eight hours later, Jonny was screaming in pain once again. The neurosurgeon then realized that we needed to insert a programmable shunt so we could adjust the settings to relieve the pressure from Jonny's head. Finally, after three different brain surgeries and shunts, this one worked. At least it worked for the time being. That in itself was a true blessing.

By February, Jonny had a feeding pump in his bedroom. By April, he had an infusion pump for the saline flushes, which were part of the chemotherapy. And then he got a morphine pump and more surgeries. We'd set up a four-tiered shelving unit for all of the odds and ends needed to take care of Jonny: alcohol pads, saline flushes, Heparin flushes, and on and on. I started as a person that would faint at the smell of an alcohol pad to a mom who used them daily to wash Jonny's port extension. I became quite the nurse, Jonny and family would say. Every time I opened the refrigerator, I'd see Jonny's morphine and Ativan bottles. Various other drugs were scattered across the countertop. It was impossible to walk into our house and not realize that something was very wrong.

Of course, all of this became our "new normal," and Jonny, Jacky, Jon, and I all rearranged our lives around the cancer treatments and Jonny's health. But in those early days, immediately after the diagnosis and surgery, what held our family together was our faith. In many ways, "normal" was just another word for "the plan." "Getting back to normal" was just another way of imagining that our lives would somehow return to the plans that we'd made for ourselves. In those early days, we still prayed that Jonny would experience a full recovery, that the radiation treatments and chemotherapy would be all that was needed and that the side effects would fade away or at least not be that bad. We prayed that God would return us to the plans we had for our lives, accepting that we might need to make some minor adjustments but still knowing that it was fully God's will to do just that.

But we also prayed for the strength to make it through this process. And while a full recovery was not a prayer that God granted, He did provide us with the strength to endure these hardships. I am surprised at the strength I found in myself in the months that followed, the strength my husband showed in his support for all of us, and even the strength that Jacky displayed. But most of all, I am still amazed at the courage and faith that Jonny maintained through all of the tests, treatments, and setbacks he faced. I think we expect such little strength from children for the simple reason that we seldom heap that much trouble on them. But I would learn in the coming year that true strength can be found at the most unlikely times and in the most unlikely places.

Chapter 4
All about the Posts

A story has been floating around for years, a modern-day parable that's been called the parable of the flood, the parable of the drowning man, or the parable of the rowboat. If you're not familiar with it, the basic premise is that a devout man is told that a storm is coming and his neighborhood will soon be flooded. His neighbor offers him a ride to safety in his truck, but the devout man refuses, stating that God will save him from harm. The storm comes and the neighborhood floods. The devout man finds himself trapped on the second floor of his house as the floodwaters continue to rise. A man in a rowboat approaches him and offers him a ride to safety. Again, the devout man refuses, stating that God will save him from harm. Finally, the floodwaters have risen so high that the devout man finds himself on the roof. A helicopter circles his house and a ladder is dropped for him to climb to safety, but again the devout man states that God will save him. Eventually, the man drowns. When he finds himself in heaven, he asks God why He never came to save him, to which God responds, "I sent you a truck, then a rowboat, then a helicopter. What more did you expect?"

I never expected God to open the skies and magically take the cancer out of Jonny. I knew that whatever help He provided would be through people. Of course, I expected a number of doctors and nurses to be involved. I expected my immediate family and close friends to lend moral support. But no way could I have known how many people were going to join us in this struggle.

I began posting about Jonny's cancer diagnosis on Facebook almost immediately. And from the beginning, I knew that Jonny would not be alone. Jon, Jacky, and I were all there with him from the start, and we were the first members of "Team Jonny." I began using the hashtag #teamjonny in my posts to drive that point home.

My daughter came up with the idea to create a separate Facebook page for Team Jonny. The page was made on December 28, 2014, two days after he was diagnosed, and within a week it had 3,600 followers. At first, she would simply repost what I wrote on my personal Facebook page to the Team Jonny page, but eventually I began posting to the new page directly. Over the next year, the following on

"Send me butterflies"

the Team Jonny page has slowly risen and, as of this writing, it's nearing 70,000 followers.

I'm sure many of the people who chose to follow this page didn't think too much about it at first. If they posted a prayer or a story about their own struggle with cancer, they may have wondered if I even read them. But I did read them. I read everything that these thousands of supporters sent to me, and I will never forget how many strangers reached out to someone in pain to offer comfort. I no longer even think of them as strangers. I've been told more than a thousand times that people feel as if they know me after reading my many posts. My answer is always, "You do know me." If you're reading this book because you followed my posts on Facebook, then not only do you know me already, but you've already helped me through the worst hardship I've ever faced. I can never thank you enough for that.

But it takes more than moral support to fight cancer. Quite frankly, it takes money. Like that devout man waiting on his rooftop, at first I assumed that God would provide what was needed. And like that devout man, God provided by sending friends and family members with fund-raising ideas.

In my spare time—back when I had "spare time"—I would bake cookies for people who were ill and in hospitals. Several of us made these specially decorated cookies from a group known as Cookie Hugs. I'd told the other "cookiers" about what was happening with Jonny. They felt the desperate need to help. Several of them had experience with cancer treatment costs and knew how expensive it could get. So, on their own, they set up a GoFundMe page. Like the Facebook page, I was amazed at the amount of supporters it attracted. And my friends at Cookie Hugs were right: cancer treatment was expensive, and this page helped us a great deal in coping with those costs.

People began to ask about purchasing T-shirts to help fund-raise. My sister, Kristine, began a CafePress shop on February 7, 2015. Her idea was to place Jonny's own drawings and the Team Jonny logo on T-shirts and other items. Again, I didn't expect much to come from it, but Jonny loved the idea, and I was grateful that people were trying to help. Well, being an artist herself, Kristine not only knew the value of art, but she knew a thing or two about how to market Jonny's artwork. Jonny's first commission paycheck for his drawings was $637. He was so surprised! So was I.

It's easy to feel abandoned by God in times of trouble. But how could I ever feel abandoned? God had sent people to the hospital and thousands of Facebook followers online. He'd sent me donations through GoFundMe. He'd sent me doctors and nurses to treat my son. He'd sent me a family and

"Send me butterflies"

my mom, Darlene, to walk beside me through every day of this struggle. He'd sent me friends who thought of financial concerns when I was too preoccupied to do so. He'd even sent Jonny his very own paycheck through CafePress. What more could I expect?

Of course, help isn't always offered spontaneously. Sometimes we have to ask for it. That's a lot more difficult than many people realize. Most of us are so accustomed to thinking of ourselves as self-sufficient that we might consider asking for help to be a sign of weakness, rather than a sign of humility. Jon displayed both humility and strength when he sent the following letter to the Jersey County Journal. And, once again, we were overwhelmed by the response.

1.22.15 – Open letter from the Wade Family

Thirty days ago, everything was perfect in our house. We prepared for Christmas with anticipation and excitement; fully expecting a magical season as only 7 year olds can experience it.

A week before Christmas, Jonny got a headache at school. The day after Christmas he was diagnosed with a malignant brain tumor and underwent a 5-hour surgery to remove as much of the tumor as possible. In the span of a week, our full hearts were drained and crushed. Our happiness became despair, our strength was exposed for its weakness, and our faith evaporated away...leaving behind only fear and worry.

We had nothing left in us as we waited for news from the surgery that night. We prayed to God for strength and healing...and soon we heard a light knock on the door. God's strength walked into our waiting room. The Weber's and Eschbach's had come by to see us. Our phones began to ring, beep and vibrate. It was God's strength contacting us at all hours of the day and night. His strength was already driving in from Missouri and had caught the first flight from Florida.

Since that horrible day, God's love has blown up our phone with messages. We have found it in our mailbox. It is delivered to our door on a daily basis. We saw it in our churches and schools, in restaurants and at work. It's shown to us everywhere we go. It is inescapable, undeniable, and overwhelming. We prayed for strength ... and God gave us you.

You have embraced us as a family in ways that I still can't believe when I think about it. You have loved our son as your own.

"Send me butterflies"

Your prayers and petitions have sustained us when we couldn't go on anymore. In the last few days Jonny has endured four brain surgeries, multiple IV sticks, a surgical port placement, spinal taps, multiple spinal headaches from high brain pressures, and the general ickiness you get from spending your winter break in the hospital. Through all this, God has matched the depth of our heartache, in equal measure, with the love you have shown us. I believe your actions, whatever they were, to be divinely inspired to give us exactly what we needed exactly when we needed it.

We can never repay you for what you have done for us. All I hope to express is that your words and deeds have touched us deeply and given us strength. We are honored to call you our friends.

I know the many prayers for Jonny's healing have been heard as well, and the answer to those prayers is already in progress in ways I can't yet see or discern. I would ask those so inclined to also pray that Jonny be spared the horrible side effects of the treatments he is getting ready to start. If nothing else, Jonny's cancer has cured me of my weak faith and my over-confidence in my own strength.

I believe we are accountable and judged by God, not only as individuals but also as groups when we organize. It doesn't matter if that organization is a nation, a church, a city, a company, a family, or a sports team. With that in mind, I close my letter by praying God's blessings on you and your organization in tangible ways that reflect and honor the love you have shown me and my family.

Go TeamJonny!

Jon, Kimberly, Kayla, Jonny and Jacky

Chapter 5
Jumped the Gun

The basic aim of radiation treatment is to use high doses of radiation to kill living cells, both cancerous and normal. The ultimate goal is to save as many of the normal cells and kill as many of the cancerous cells as possible. Jonny hated going for his radiation treatments. It involved an hour-long drive to the hospital, followed by various delays due to equipment failures and scheduling mix-ups, so that the twenty-minute radiation treatment itself would often end up taking close to the entire day.

He started vomiting immediately after the treatments began and never stopped; my son would throw up almost daily for the rest of his life, even months after the treatments had been completed. On top of that, I had to keep him sedated for the procedures, which left him feeling groggy and cranky when he finally woke up. Eventually, Jonny would be taking seventeen different medications, including oxycodone and valium, on a daily basis to give him relief from his pain and relax his muscles. My son would often beg me not to take him for the radiation treatments, but what choice did I have? How could I not?

Besides the nausea and grogginess, the radiation treatments also burned him. To be clear, this wasn't a "burning sensation" that he experienced after each treatment. He had literal third-degree burns on his entire head and all down his spine. Eventually, after his hair fell out, I began rubbing burn lotion on his head and back every day to try to reduce the pain.

It was all I could do. My son had cancer, and all I could do was make sure he took his seventeen different medications on schedule, drive him to and from the radiation treatments that he dreaded, empty the vomit bucket, have peppermint oil for him to smell for his nausea, and rub lotion on his burns. It was a lot of work, but it didn't seem to make him feel better. I couldn't stop his vomiting. I couldn't stop the burning. I couldn't make the cancer go away.

All any of us could do were little things to make life easier for Jonny. Despite the burning, the radiation treatments often left Jonny feeling cold, so Jon and I bought a different car in April, one with heated backseats so our son could stay warm during his many trips to the hospital. Even Jacky found little ways to help his brother get through this ordeal, and one of his ideas truly surprised me.

"Send me butterflies"

We'd been told about the radiation treatments and the effects they would have on Jonny. We knew his hair would fall out, and this detail seemed to especially trouble Jacky. So on January 24, weeks before Jonny's hair began coming out in clumps, Jacky decided to shave his own head so Jonny wouldn't feel alone. Keep in mind, they were twins. They were never alone. Never.

I can't say enough times how proud I am of both my sons. Jon was just as proud, to the point where he decided to do the same thing. It made Jonny feel so good that we were all in this together. Jonny let me off the hook from shaving my head, saying that since I was a girl, I'd better keep my hair.

In fact, Jonny didn't begin to lose his hair until February 11, some three weeks after Jacky and Jon had shaved their heads. At that point, he'd said to me, "They jumped the gun a little, I'd say."

Here was my son, cracking jokes while fighting cancer, as he'd always done before. Then my other son, doing anything he could think of to make sure his brother didn't feel alone. My husband, not just nodding in approval, but joining wholeheartedly in supporting both our sons. That's our family. That's our Team Jonny.

During his treatment while in first grade, he only attended five months of the school year. Before moving him on to second grade, his elementary school teacher suggested we test him after I voiced my concern about the side effects of the radiation. We were told that the high dose of radiation he received would decrease his intelligence significantly. Although I didn't see any of this, I was concerned about it. They administered the test and Jonny tested at a fourth-grade level. Jonny wasn't smart; he was brilliant.

Chapter 6
All the Support

I've already mentioned Facebook, CafePress, and GoFundMe and the phenomenal response we received through setting up each of these sites. But sometimes people reached out to us without our even having to ask, and I wanted to share a few words about them as well.

Immediately after Jonny was diagnosed with cancer, we were contacted by Jen Rogers about the Make-A-Wish Foundation. Of course, at the time I'm sure that I could have been more gracious (this was on December 26, literally hours after being told that my son had a brain tumor), but Jen said that she'd like to work on making a wish of Jonny's come true. Obviously, the first wish any child with cancer will make is to no longer have cancer. And while that wasn't something that Jen could offer, the Make-A-Wish Foundation has been working for decades to help bring joy and comfort to children who have to endure more hardship than any child should ever have to endure.

Jonny's wish? He wanted to go shark fishing in Hawaii. If you've visited our CafePress site—the one with Jonny's drawings on it—you'll know that he was fascinated with sharks. I don't know if Jonny had ever heard that sharks were immune to cancer, but it is a common—although completely false—belief about sharks. Jen said she would look into it and let us know.

I can't say that I gave the Make-A-Wish Foundation much thought over the next few months, as treating my son's cancer was always foremost in my mind. But on March 13, we received a call from Jen, telling us that the foundation would grant Jonny's wish. They would arrange and pay for a trip to Hawaii, as well as arrange for the shark fishing expedition. Unfortunately, due to Jonny's radiation treatments and subsequent chemotherapy schedule, he wouldn't be able to go until the winter, but he was still excited about the news. So even though Jonny never did get the chance to go on the actual shark fishing trip, the Make-A-Wish Foundation still managed to bring my son joy through a difficult time in his life, and I am grateful to them for that.

In addition to the Make-A-Wish Foundation, a number of local celebrities took time out from their schedules to visit Jonny. And some of them ended up doing a lot more than simply visit.

"Send me butterflies"

After attending a hockey game on March 31, Jonny and Jacky got to meet with St. Louis Blues player Alex Steen. He took some time to play a quick game with both my sons, give them each a goodie bag with their very own Steen jerseys, as well as give them a tour of the facilities. He took his time and showed how much he cared.

On July 29, John Lackey, a pitcher for the St. Louis Cardinals, showed up at the hospital with his wife. They stayed for about twenty minutes, chatting with us about random subjects. At one point, Mr. Lackey took the cap off his head, signed it, and gave it to Jonny. Jonny fussed a bit in adjusting the cap so it didn't fall past his ears and cover half his face. At one point, I was able to catch a wonderful photograph of Mr. Lackey and Jonny both laughing as the hat fell past his eyes. When John found out that we planned on attending one of his games, he told Jonny he'd make sure to bring out some of the other players to meet him and Jacky after the game. However, when that Friday came, John Lackey did much more than that. He asked my husband to bring both the boys into the locker room where all the players were. John took them around to each player and introduced them. He also gave both the boys a hat and a baseball autographed by every player on the team. Both boys were so excited. Jonny made a funny joke about one of the players being in his underwear when Jonny met him.

On September 7, Jonny got a visit from Lt. Abby Moody of the United States Army. She presented Jonny with a United States flag, a challenge coin, a certificate, and a couple of knit hats. For those who don't know, challenge coins have been around for nearly a century and are given to recognize special achievement in times of great challenge. She then told Jonny that her unit had flown the flag she was giving him over their base in Alaska in a show of support. Jonny, as usual, was grateful and enjoyed the hats she brought with her, too.

The next day, Adam Martin from the Seattle Mariners Double A team came to visit. He brought autographed bats for both Jonny and Jacky (I'm always grateful when well-wishers remember to think of both my sons), as well as baseball cards and autographed balls. After meeting with Jonny and Jacky, Adam agreed to meet with the rest of the boys' baseball team. He spent over an hour signing baseballs, answering questions, and posing for pictures. After Adam left, I was speaking with Jonny about how I'd arranged for his whole team to meet with Adam, and Jonny told me, "I'm glad it's not just me! It should be all of us!" Jonny always thought of others first, and this was no exception.

"Send me butterflies"

Shelby Miller had been a pitcher for the St. Louis Cardinals and was currently a pitcher for the Atlanta Braves. He and his wife, Amy, arranged for a benefit poker run to raise money for Jonny's hospital costs. On October 17, Shelby sold autographed photographs of himself, poker hands, and drink coolers, with all of the proceeds going toward Jonny's medical bills. Later that weekend, Shelby drove to visit Jonny in the hospital since we weren't able to attend the Poker Run. Jonny immediately noticed that Shelby was wearing a cross around his neck similar to Jonny's. Jonny took his out from under his shirt and showed Shelby, commenting that they had the same one. Shelby came over and sat next to Jonny on his hospital bed to compare. Jonny thought it was pretty special that Shelby wore a cross and never took it off, just like him.

Pat Fallon, Texas State Representative, was introduced to Jonny's story from a friend who lived in the neighborhood. Although he didn't want to read the sad posts, he did one day. It moved him so much that he decided to do something to raise awareness and funds for pediatric cancer. And, like they say in Texas, he went big. He decided to enter the 777 World Marathon Challenge, a challenge that takes the participants to seven different continents in seven days to run seven marathons. Usually only ultra-athletes entered such a marathon, which Pat was not. Pat had never run a marathon in his life and had only a couple months to train. Yes, Pat finishing this challenge would take a miracle, and a miracle is what he found. Pat speaks about "feeling Jonny" during several of the marathons when he felt he couldn't take one more step. Pat went on to complete this 777 World Marathon Challenge, getting his best time in his last marathon.

So many other individuals and organizations took the time to visit with Jonny, help raise funds for his treatment, and raise awareness about Jonny's struggle and the struggle of all children coping with pediatric cancer—the St. Louis Rams, the New England Patriots, the West Plains Grizzlies, and on and on. It's always wonderful to see how difficult times can bring out the best in people, awakening a desire to help in whatever way they can.

One night, while my husband was tucking Jonny into bed, he asked, "What do you think about people stopping by and sending you cards just to meet you?"

Jonny's reply was simply, "It makes me feel like I'm not alone."

For everyone who visited Jonny, at home, in the hospital, at various events, I want to thank you all. For everyone who sent Jonny cards and e-mails, I want to thank you all. No one should ever have to suffer alone, especially a child. And thanks to every one of you, no matter how bad things got, my son always knew that he was never alone and always loved.

Chapter 7
God Appears

One of the struggles we face in accepting God's plan for us is that it's often difficult to figure out what that plan is. We may try to follow the path He's laid out for us, but we'll always have that nagging doubt that we've lost our way or that we've completely misunderstood the plan. At those times, if we learn to listen, we can hear God's voice guiding us. If we keep ourselves open, we can feel the presence of God in our lives.

Of course, sometimes God's presence is neither subtle nor quiet. On May 22, while we were in for a round of chemotherapy treatment, I was getting ready for bed when I noticed Jonny crying as I stood at the hospital sink. When I quickly turned to have a seat next to him, I couldn't help but wonder what had happened now. Was he in pain? Was he nauseous? Was he scared? After five months of cancer treatment, what more could possibly happen to him?

But when I saw him, he didn't seem afraid. When I asked him what was wrong, he said, "Nothing. It's about God."

Then he began crying harder. I asked him if he was upset. Although I'd placed my faith in God to see us through this hardship, committing myself to accept His plan, Jonny was still only eight years old. Maybe he thought he was being punished by God or even that he'd been abandoned by God; a lot of people in his situation would.

But Jonny shook his head and said, "No." He wasn't upset. When I asked if he felt happy, he said, "Yes."

He'd also been listening to Christian music on his headphones, which helped since his hearing was already deteriorating. I tried to explain to him that what was happening was that he felt touched by God. I was at peace and happy that God would remind us both of His presence, that He still watched over us all and that this was indeed a part of His greater plan.

But Jonny shook his head again. "No, it's more than that. He's here!" He then told me that he needed to speak to Him, closed his eyes, and began to pray. I panicked inside even though I wanted to be delighted. Was God ready to take my son home? I started to plead with God that if this was His plan, to not take Jonny while I was alone at the hospital. "Please don't take him right now. I'm not strong enough to do it on my own!" I prayed. Eventually, Jonny took hold of my hand

"Send me butterflies"

and began to cry again, saying, "God makes me feel special, and I like to feel special." Then he said, "I want to see him."

You can imagine that this statement left me even more concerned. "Seeing God" is often a euphemism for dying. Rather than trying to dissuade Jonny, I instead tried to reassure him with tears running down my face, "In time, honey, in time. You can talk to Him, though."

But Jonny became insistent. "No, I need to see Him face-to-face." Then he went on to say, "He's done everything for me. He helps me get through this. He even had His son die on the cross for me. He loves me so much. All I keep saying is, 'Thank you, thank you, thank you.' I love Him. I want to be baptized on Sunday. Can I, Mom?"

That evening, after the experience, I jotted everything down so I could share it with my husband. The next morning, I told Jon and my mother about what Jonny had said, and we all agreed that a baptism was a great idea. But Jon also had something to share with me. For the first time in his life, Jon had fasted the day before. During this fasting, Jon asked that God be present to Jonny. Jon and I both looked at each other in awe. God came to comfort our son as Jon had asked.

Jon spoke to Jonny about what he'd experienced, and Jonny tried to explain as best he could manage that, while he couldn't see God, he could feel God's presence at his bedside. And while God didn't speak to him, Jonny had been speaking with God. My husband and son then shared a prayer of salvation, and we decided he would be baptized a week later when our hospital stay was over.

On May 31, we gathered at the First Baptist Church of Jerseyville for Jonny's baptism. Despite being weak and a little scared, my son was determined to go through with the baptism. Jon shared the story of how Jonny had come to this decision and went on to say the following:

> I'm praising God for the blessing of our family.
>
> As the father of two boys, I have always had big hopes and dreams for their future. It is the prerogative of fathers to dream for their sons. Jonny, in particular, has always been special, with physical and mental gifts that have impressed both his parents since he was a baby.
>
> Since his diagnosis of cancer and our understanding of it, I have grieved our loss of normalcy. I have grieved my loss of the hopes and dreams I had for his future. Where I once imagined a valedictorian . . . the doctors warned of tutors and late-night homework sessions that might be very frustrating. Where I once imagined

"Send me butterflies"

a star pitcher . . . the doctors warned of braces, wheelchairs, and unsteady coordination.

God then taught me a lesson. First, that I had no right to those hopes and dreams, because the things I thought were mine were really God's. Second, Jonny belongs to God, and He can and will provide for him with or without me. Jonny's future—how many days he has and what he does with them—belongs to God. I'm just lucky enough to be his caretaker while he is here and have no right to plan his future or presume his number of days upon the earth.

After coming to terms with this, I see how God has blessed me with a father's pride in his son anyway. And beyond what I could have imagined before his diagnosis. How many fathers can say this?

My son has been contacted by every professional sports team near his hometown to honor him in some way: the St. Louis Cardinals, St. Louis Blues, and St. Louis Rams.

He has also been honored by the Seattle Mariners, New England Patriots, and West Plains Grizzlies.

Kimberly Denise Wade

My son has been repeatedly sought out by heads of state, professional athletes, and media outlets to discuss his story. He has been featured on the House floor and invited as an honoree at the State of the Union Address for his courage and selflessness.

My son has been sought out by companies to endorse their products and by charities to endorse their events.

My son has led parades that honor him and his battles.

My son has cool scars, and all the girls want to be near him to hear him tell his stories.

My son has received two proclamations from the state of Illinois and one from the state of Texas recognizing his courage and bravery in the face of adversity.

My son has a fan club that spans the world. He is known throughout many communities as if he is a rock star . . . and he is only eight years old.

I don't know any other dad that can say that about their son. I tell him how proud I am of him all the time. He just smiles back and tells me he

"Send me butterflies"

loves me. That alone makes me the proudest papa on the planet.

I've grieved the life I dreamed for him as his father, and God has given back so much more than I could have imagined. Much of this happened via the unlikely pathway of his mother, her cell phone, and Facebook. Praise God—for working through his mother—to do all this for us.

While I was so proud of both of them and could see that many in the congregation were moved by Jonny's story, I should have known that my son wouldn't let the mood remain too serious for too long. After the baptism, he said, "That was some dunk! But I think God is happy!" I think God was happy on that day as well.

As the months went by, Jonny didn't lose his faith in God or the comfort from knowing that God was never far from his side. He would often talk about God's plan for him, speaking of his cancer not as a curse or punishment, but simply as one element in a far grander plan that none of us could fully understand. It often reminded me of the poem "The Brave Little Soul" by John Alessi.

Not too long ago in Heaven there was a little soul who took wonder in observing the world. He especially enjoyed the love he saw there and often expressed this joy with God. One day however the little soul was sad, for on this day he saw suffering in the world. He approached God and sadly asked, "Why do bad things happen; why is there suffering in the world?" God paused for a moment and replied, "Little soul, do not be sad, for the suffering you see, unlocks the love in people's hearts." The little soul was confused. "What do you mean," he asked. God replied, "Have you not noticed the goodness and love that is the offspring of that suffering? Look at how people come together, drop their differences and show their love and compassion for those who suffer. All their other motivations disappear and they become motivated by love alone." The little soul began to understand and listened attentively as God continued, "The suffering soul unlocks the love in people's hearts much like the sun and the rain unlock the flower within the seed. I created everyone with endless love in their heart, but unfortunately most people keep it locked up and hardly share it with anyone. They are afraid to let their love shine freely, because they are afraid

"Send me butterflies"

of being hurt. But a suffering soul unlocks that love. I tell you this - it is the greatest miracle of all. Many souls have bravely chosen to go into the world and suffer - to unlock this love - to create this miracle for the good of all humanity."

Just then the little soul got a wonderful idea and could hardly contain himself. With his wings fluttering, bouncing up and down, the little soul excitedly replied. "I am brave; let me go! I would like to go into the world and suffer so that I can unlock the goodness and love in people's hearts! I want to create that miracle!" God smiled and said, "You are a brave soul I know, and thus I will grant your request. But even though you are very brave you will not be able to do this alone. I have known since the beginning of time that you would ask for this and so I have carefully selected many souls to care for you on your journey. Those souls will help you create your miracle; however they will also share in your suffering. Two of these souls are most special and will care for you, help you and suffer along with you, far beyond the others. They have already chosen a name for you." God and the brave soul shared a smile, and then embraced.

In parting, God said, "Do not forget little soul that I will be with you always. Although you have agreed to bear the pain, you will do so through my strength. And if the time should come when you feel that you have suffered enough, just say the word, think the thought, and you will be healed." Thus at that moment the brave little soul was born into the world, and through his suffering and God's strength, he unlocked the goodness and love in people's hearts. For so many people dropped their differences and came together to show their love. Priorities became properly aligned. People gave from their hearts. Those that were always too busy found time. Many began new spiritual journeys, some regained lost faith - many came back to God. Parents hugged their children tighter. Friends and family grew closer. Old friends got together and new friendships were made. Distant family reunited, and every family spent more time together. Everyone prayed. Peace and love reigned. Lives changed forever. It was good. The world was a better place. The miracle had happened. God was pleased.

"Send me butterflies"

I've gone on about so many of the people who helped Jonny through this ordeal, but I never want to forget that each of us were only with him part of the time. We each had other things to do. Jacky had school. Jon had his job. I couldn't be by Jonny's side every minute of the day even though I tried. And we all had to sleep once in a while. But one presence stayed by my son's side through every moment of his struggle, offering comfort even if none of us could see or hear Him.

Chapter 8
A Piece at a Time

Our plan was to see Jonny through the cancer, deal with short-term hardships, and eventually get our son back the way he was before the whole ugly thing began. Of course, he might need to take some medication long term, maybe have some types of food he wouldn't be able to eat, or even have scarring from the radiation treatment and surgery. But the healthy, active boy we'd known two weeks before Christmas would return to us, sooner or later. We'd treated cancer like a dark journey that we would go on together but come out unharmed for the most part.

But every journey leads to a new place, and you never end up exactly where you began.

As the months went by, it became obvious that Jonny was not going to emerge from this cancer the same as he'd been. Cancer isn't an all-or-nothing condition, and it's more than just a gradual weakening. Cancer takes you a piece at a time, sometimes small pieces and sometimes large. Even the treatments take pieces of you away, as if trading them in exchange for a longer life.

The first and most obvious sign of this "taking away" was my son's weight loss. Between the two-dozen-plus medications, half-dozen surgeries, radiation treatments, chemotherapy, and endless tests, Jonny never had much of an appetite. I've mentioned the daily episodes of vomiting. Imagine how hungry you feel after vomiting; now imagine feeling that way every day. Not only was it difficult for Jonny to hold in food long enough to digest nutrients, but most of the time he didn't want to eat. Anyone who followed my Facebook posts through 2015 might remember the genuine excitement I felt when my son not only finished but kept down a full hamburger, hot dog, or sandwich. Eventually, a "G-button"—G for gastronomic—had to be placed in his stomach so he could be fed nightly through a pump. But that didn't stop the vomiting. Most of the time, after the pump had run slowly all night long, Jonny would wake up and immediately vomit. So the first way the cancer took away Jonny was by slowly reducing his weight so there was literally less of him every day.

Of course, the lack of nutrients and the damage done by radiation treatment would affect Jonny's muscles. Eventually, his legs grew so weak that the doctors said he would need leg braces if he recovered. If you have a child, then you're no

"Send me butterflies"

doubt familiar with their boundless energy, and Jonny had tons of it. Jonny loved to run, ride his bike, and would often ride his scooter around the house when it was too chilly to ride it outside. Jonny was athletic. One of Jonny's favorite things to do while watching television with the family was to practice the perfect headstand. He would say, "Mom, watch this one!" over and over again. He got good at them, but Jonny was good at almost everything.

Jonny had the balance and the skills to ride a bike after one lesson. That is the main reason it was so difficult when he couldn't do those things anymore. He longed to be able to run again and be the fastest one like he used to be. He longed to do his awesome headstands that he practiced for years on. He longed to ride his scooter but no longer had the balance or energy needed for any of the things he used to do.

Generally, as soon as a child learns how to walk, he or she starts running and doesn't stop for years. It's tiresome keeping up with a little boy who's filled with an endless supply of energy, and I was often amazed at how fast someone could move with such small legs. If you're like me, you've probably wished more than once that your children would just slow down once in a while. But during the year that Jonny had cancer, I would have given anything to see him running through our house again. I would have given anything to find out that my boy had skinned his knee while riding his bike or broken his hand while playing football; after cancer, those would have been great days in comparison. Instead, I'd been told that he would need braces to walk, assuming that he could beat the cancer. Any plans our son might have had for being on a baseball team, football team, or basketball team were gone.

After Jonny's first chemotherapy treatment, he suffered a 25% hearing loss. We were told that the hearing loss would be permanent. After the second chemotherapy treatment, he'd lost over 50% of his hearing. By the end of his treatments, Jonny was on the borderline of needing a hearing aid. Maybe that seems minor, but try walking down a street while wearing a pair of earplugs and you'll quickly realize how disconnected you feel from the rest of the world without your full hearing. My son would have to strain to follow conversations, music, television shows, and movies for the rest of his life.

The various treatments Jonny was undergoing had also resulted in some loss of vision. He required several surgeries for one of his eyes. Although he could still see through both eyes, the brain surgeries had done lasting damage, and we were told he would suffer from a permanent reduction in depth perception. Again, if that doesn't sound like a big deal, try walking down a street with a patch over one eye. A list

"Send me butterflies"

of future school activities and careers were now closed off to my son. He had a better than average chance to never be able to even drive a car.

It probably won't surprise you to know that Jonny's favorite verse in the Bible came from the book of Job. I'm sure he could see quite a lot of himself in the character of Job, a man who was tested by God, not because of any wrongdoing he'd committed, but because God wanted to use him as an example of true faith. Despite Job's many hardships and setbacks, he proved Satan wrong every day that he refused to renounce God. As Jonny was losing weight, the use of his legs, his hearing, and his sight, he'd chosen to be baptized. As the cancer took away more pieces of him, he would remember Job 23:10: "Yet he knows the way I have taken; when he has tested me, I will emerge as pure gold."

And the truth is that my son did emerge as pure gold, despite all that he'd lost. His faith never faltered and, in fact, grew stronger as time wore on. While everyone else was trying to comfort my son, he was looking past his own suffering and trying to find a way to make it into something positive. During the first two weeks following Jonny's diagnosis, I would often question why God had chosen to inflict so much suffering on my son, always with the understanding that this wasn't part of the "deal" I had with God. That deal, of course, was that I would maintain loyalty to God, and He would, in turn, make sure that life went according to my plan. Of course, I came to accept that God's plan was not my own and that I should place my trust in His will, but it was difficult. How much more difficult was it for Jonny, only eight years old and slowly slipping away a piece at a time, to understand that God had His own plan and that we needed to accept that? And yet he did, never straying from his faith.

One day, I was driving Jonny to a clinic appointment at the children's hospital, his least favorite thing to do. We had just left the city limits of Jerseyville when Jonny said, "Mom, I can't get this song out of my head." Well, being the music lover Jonny was, I thought it was a top 10 song he was speaking about.

I asked, "What song?"

Jonny said in his ever so sweet voice, "I keep singing 'When I die, I'm gonna fly, fly, fly.'" My eyes filled with tears as I drove. He then said, "I don't know why people think of it as a sad thing. I think of it as a joyous thing!"

Fighting back the crackling in my voice, I said, "Jonny, it is a joyous thing. We should all want to go to heaven." I couldn't think straight to offer any more, which I regret. He continued to sing that line a couple more times before he

"Send me butterflies" was off onto another subject. I can still hear him singing it to this day.

Sometimes it seems as if, the more pieces of Jonny's body the cancer stripped away, the more his inner spirit was revealed. And while I had always assumed it was God's plan that I teach my son right from wrong and what was important in life, I found that my son had just as much to teach me.

Chapter 9
Twin Brothers

As you get older, you hopefully understand that your ideas about how the world should work and the realities of how the world actually works won't always match. When you're seven years old, it's far more difficult to accept or even to understand.

Jackson is Jonny's twin brother and, like most twins, they began building separate identities for themselves at a young age. Jackson resembled Jon, and Jonny was my mini me. Jackson was always more quiet and introspective than Jonny. Even his nickname, Jacky, was Jonny's idea.

By the age of seven, Jacky was already a perfectionist and highly competitive. He also tended to worry about new situations and new places. If we were going to be separated for any reason, Jacky would often ask me dozens of questions about where I was going and what was going to happen before he felt comfortable leaving my side.

Jonny always had an easier time adjusting to new situations and meeting new people, and I suppose Jacky was sometimes jealous of his brother. He would often say that he had no friends, while everyone was friends with Jonny. Despite that, and despite Jacky's strong drive to compete, the two of them were best friends. But it was already obvious during their year of pre-kindergarten classes that Jacky was feeling isolated, almost as if he was being left in his popular brother's shadow.

Jon and I had discussed the matter at length and decided that, starting with kindergarten, the boys would need to be in separate classrooms. While our two boys' close friendship was wonderful, we felt Jacky building an identity of his own was important, rather than constantly comparing himself to Jonny. It was also important that Jacky make his own friends who didn't constantly compare him to his brother. After a period of adjustment, as neither of the boys wanted to be separated—even though their classrooms were right across the hall from one another—eventually Jacky became more confident and socially adjusted.

Still, I drove the boys to and from school together every day. That is, until Jonny received his cancer diagnosis. He didn't drop out of school entirely, but his attendance became far more sporadic over the year as he grew weaker and the pain became more intense. As Jacky continued to develop his friendships at school, Jonny had some understandable difficulty keeping in touch with his large circle of friends.

"Send me butterflies"

I'm sure that, like Jacky, many of the children had questions about Jonny's condition. I'm also sure that, like Jacky, most of them had little experience dealing with cancer or the possibility of death.

Of course, Jacky's time at home was also different once his brother got sick. When any parent has more than one child, he or she has to be careful not to give more attention to one than the other. This is true under the best of conditions, when "attention" is simply praising good grades. But as any parent of two or more children knows, it's impossible to always spread an equal portion of attention to one's children. Some children get into more trouble than others. Some children achieve more than others. And some children have more pressing needs than others. I could never choose between my two boys, but the fact is that one of them was fighting for his life, so that was the one I felt needed me more.

The siblings of cancer patients have to grow up more quickly than other children. They have to accept more responsibility, learn to be more independent, and be more focused on the needs of others. Jacky rose to these challenges wonderfully, and I could write a whole other book on what he's taught me about accepting God's plan for us all. But he was still only seven years old, and I could expect only so much maturity from him.

Jon and I made sure that, 90 percent of the time, Jacky was either in school or with one of us. The pattern that emerged was that I would spend a good part of the day with Jonny, whether he was at home or in the hospital. Jon would usually be with Jacky after school. We tried to at least get together as a family every day for dinner, even when that dinner was in the hospital.

It seems strange that anyone would envy a boy with a brain tumor, but over time Jacky would become resentful of the extra attention his brother was receiving. As I said, I was spending more time with Jonny than with Jacky, but of course I wasn't the only one lavishing attention on him. The Facebook group, with thousands of people offering prayers and wishing Jonny luck, congratulated him on every positive step he took. Sports figures and other celebrities visited or wrote to him. Charity events were held for him. Students and teachers worried over Jonny and frequently asked Jacky how his brother was doing. Even in his own classroom, even without his brother right across the hall, it's easy to see that Jacky's identity was still being overshadowed by Jonny's. He'd become "that boy whose brother had cancer."

It shouldn't have been a surprise when Jacky once said that he wished he had cancer too. He certainly understood the seriousness of Jonny's condition, but his own need for

"Send me butterflies"

attention was strong as well. Of course, resenting the attention that someone else receives in a time of crisis is immature, but Jacky was seven. He was at the age when he should have been immature. But Jonny's cancer forced him to grow up faster than any boy should.

Since they were twins, it was sometimes difficult for me to watch the two boys standing side by side. They were fraternal twins, so obviously they were never mirror images of one another, but they were the same age and clearly resembled one another. True, Jacky was becoming different from Jonny as far as personalities went, yet physically they were supposed to be similar. But when I saw them together, one boy was strong and healthy, while the other was wasting away. It was as if I could see all of the potential still left in one boy's future, while I watched the other's options slowly narrow down to one. This took a part of my soul that I would never regain again.

But Jacky also reminds of something far more important. Despite all of the loss I've suffered, I am still blessed with a wonderful son, a son who has grown into a person who resembles both him and his brother. Jacky is now a witty, fun, loving, brave child himself. He makes himself do things he would have resisted or refused to do previously. He is finding himself slowly developing into an incredible boy that I'm deeply proud of and who is teaching me that we must move forward little by little, one step at a time.

Chapter 10
Mr. Wonderful

Cancer can destroy so much more than bodies. I've already gone on about how it slowly destroyed my plans for Jonny's future. Cancer can also destroy your faith in God. Cancer can destroy the optimism it takes to just get out of bed every morning. Cancer can make you feel helpless, and it can make you resent the people around you, who are also helpless. It can also destroy marriages.

A week after Jonny's diagnosis, Jon and I spoke with a social worker about some of the long-term effects of cancer that most people don't consider. She let us know that 50% of couples that have a child with cancer end up getting divorced, and 75% go bankrupt. It's one of the most stressful situations a couple can endure. You worry about your child's health and safety, coupled with the additional expenses that come with cancer treatment, all of the extra time spent taking care of that child, and the temptation to blame somebody for what's happening. Objectively, it's ridiculous to blame a spouse for a child's cancer, but emotion can beat reason during hard times.

We were then told that the 50% divorce rate applies only to couples when the child recovers from cancer. For couples whose children have died from cancer—or, I imagine, any number of other conditions—that divorce rate spikes to above 90%. What this social worker was telling us was that, if Jonny didn't beat his cancer, our marriage had only a one in ten chance of surviving. Again, take all of the emotional turmoil of taking care of a child with cancer and add to it the depression and anger of losing that child. On top of that, after all that you and your spouse have gone through together, he or she will end up being a reminder of the child you lost. What this means is, even if your husband or wife is by your side during every day of this ordeal, that constant support might end up making him or her a reminder of your loss and make divorce even more likely.

Obviously, the social worker was not suggesting that our marriage was weak or that there was anything wrong with Jon or me. She was merely pointing out that even the strongest marriages would be tested by the loss of a child or even the risk of losing a child. It's easy to become so laser-focused on a sick child that we forget to take care of ourselves and other people. I'm sure that many people assumed Jonny would become my entire world once he was diagnosed. But

"Send me butterflies"

the fact is that this experience has brought me closer to so many other people, including my husband and Jacky.

Jon wasn't able to spend as much face-to-face time with Jonny during his final year because of his job. Still, he always managed to make time not only for Jonny and Jacky, but also for me. Despite the amazing insights both of our sons shared with us, they were still children, and at times we both needed to speak with an adult about adult concerns. I've shared a great deal with my Facebook community, but some moments I couldn't bring myself to share with the world. And while I never lied to either of my sons, I certainly put on a braver face at times than what I was truly feeling. More than anyone else, Jon saw how much this situation was tearing me apart. And more than anyone else, I saw how much it was tearing him apart.

Why are we still together, part of that elusive 10% of couples who don't get a divorce after the tragedy of losing a child? Quite simply, it's our faith in God that saw us through that horrible time, and it's our faith that continues to see us through to this day. We've both come to accept that, hard as it is to endure, Jonny's cancer was a part of God's plan, not just for Jonny, but for us as well.

I mentioned how Jon shaved his head the same day Jacky did, to show Jonny that he wasn't alone in his struggle. I mentioned how Jon would speak with doctors about Jonny's condition and our options when I couldn't bring myself to do it. I've mentioned the fund-raising events, awareness-raising events, and day-to-day activities meant to lift our son's spirits. And if I haven't always mentioned Jon's name when describing these events, please know that he was always involved, always making sure that things ran smoothly. When one of Jonny's many hospital appointments ran late, it was Jon who made sure that Jacky got picked up from school. When I needed to share my fears for the future with someone, Jon was always there to listen. Whenever things felt overwhelming, which happened a lot, I could always remind myself that I wasn't handling any of it alone. I had the strongest man I had ever known standing right next to me.

"Team Jonny" is a lot more than just a hashtag that got popular. It reflects the fact that every member of our family came together, not only to help Jonny, but also to help one another. So our marriage survived because we were able to devote ourselves to something greater than ourselves. Our marriage survived because Jonny's memory is something that strengthens that bond rather than weakens it.

Chapter 11
A Blessing of Memory Loss

I've described some of the things that my son lost due to cancer. He suffered partial loss of hearing and a partial loss of sight. He suffered a loss of mobility—he would eventually be unable to move around without the use of a walker. He experienced a dangerous level of weight loss. But for me the most difficult loss came when Jonny lost his memory.

It happened in October, after Jonny had suffered a massive seizure, the worst he would suffer. I remember this day as one of the most horrific in my life as a mother. I came home from a quick trip to the grocery store and found Jon and the boys downstairs watching a movie together. I sat down by Jonny and asked how he was feeling. He had a smile on his face and replied, "I'm tired but took a nap." He then stated that he needed to use the restroom and grabbed his walker. He assured me that he was fine to go by himself, even though I was concerned. You see, I wanted to help in every way, but also didn't want him to feel so dependent and, well, handicapped.

He returned from the bathroom, stood in front of me, and said, "I feel scared." I immediately asked why and told him to sit down next to me for us to talk about it. I cuddled him into my arms and told him that he was safe and had nothing to be afraid of. I asked him why he felt this way. He said he didn't know and stared at the TV. I repeated myself that he was safe and I was with him. I asked him several more times if the feeling had gone away but got no response. At first I thought he was just watching the movie and was no longer paying any attention to me, until I noticed he hadn't blinked for a couple minutes. I quickly got in front of him and yelled, "Jonny!" but still got no response, just a stare right through me. I panicked and yelled for help, but Jacky was the only one left downstairs. Jon had gone upstairs to get some snacks. I told Jacky to run upstairs and tell Jon it was an emergency and to call 911.

Jonny was flown to the hospital by helicopter and put on a ventilator. He was also placed in a medically induced coma, the only way the doctors could stop the miniseizures that continued to occur. He spent two weeks that way in ICU before Jon and I finally requested that he be taken out of the coma. If the doctors could do nothing more, we decided we'd prefer that he spend his final days at home, among family and familiar surroundings.

"Send me butterflies"

The irony of wanting him among familiar surroundings was that, when Jonny was first brought out of the coma, he couldn't remember us. Of course, I understood that this was a side effect of the seizures and the coma, but it was still heartbreaking to look into my son's eyes, my mini me, and know that he had no idea who I was. He was understandably afraid and immediately began praying to God. He looked at me, put his little frail hands together, and bowed his head for prayer as I stood quietly behind him with tears running down my face as if a dam had opened. I have no idea what he was praying for, as he prayed in silence, but I'm sure God was with him during that time. For the next two days, he would constantly rub the cross around his neck for comfort and pray.

After two days, he began to remember us, although the details were slow in coming. Once he looked at me and said, "I've seen you from somewhere! That building place." He couldn't even remember the hospital. Eventually, he remembered me, Jon, and even our dog Lucy. He never did remember that our other dog had passed away only a month prior and continued to ask for her. But for two days, I'd been forgotten by my own son. Even worse, he had no idea what was happening, so in addition to the pain he was suffering, he was also afraid of the people who were trying to comfort him.

Curiously, the one person Jonny never forgot was his twin brother Jacky. Not only did he always recognize Jacky, but he would often ask me about him when he wasn't in the room. He'd want to know where Jacky was, who was watching him, and when he'd be back. Because his memory was failing in other ways, Jonny would often repeat these questions multiple times, forgetting my answers minutes after I'd given them. And while he remembered his brother, he often forgot conversations they shared. At one point, he said to me, "I'm sorry I embarrass Jacky. I love him so much, but he doesn't love me." Of course, every day before Jacky went to school, he would speak with Jonny and remind him that he loved him, but he would forget these conversations as well, so we would do it every time Jacky saw Jonny.

While Jonny never again forgot his family, he had trouble remembering daily routines. His short-term memory had also been reduced to only five minutes. The seizure had damaged his short-term memory for good. What this meant was that he wouldn't know which medications he had to take at which times, which wasn't too much of a problem since I kept track of that sort of thing for him. Jonny would often praise me for becoming quite the nurse with all his medication and port flushes, etc. But it also meant that he would often forget asking for things like food or drinks. If he asked for a

"Send me butterflies"

hamburger from McDonald's, by the time I went there, got it, and brought it to him, he would have forgotten asking for it. I was always a little sad about his loss of memory, but this also meant that his life was filled with little surprises. More than once, when I'd brought him a drink or a sandwich, he would say, "You know me so well. I was just about to ask for that," having forgotten asking for it. Many times it brought a smile to his face and mine. He would start saying that I was "Wonder Woman," as I knew everything he was thinking before having to say it.

It certainly says a lot about Jonny that, even with his failing memory and the confusion that caused him, he was still worried about other people, even when he couldn't remember their names or how he knew them. It's the same compassion that would lead him to wonder how he could help other children suffering from cancer, using his suffering to help others. It's the same compassion that shined through even as my son lost everything else that made him Jonny.

But even through this terrible loss was one positive side effect, a silver lining in a dark cloud. Jonny seemed to have lost almost all memory of the year he'd spent fighting cancer. The horrible radiation treatments that had burned him and the chemotherapy that had left him vomiting multiple times per day were forgotten. The various operations and painful recoveries were forgotten. Those long stays in the hospital were forgotten. By the end, all he knew was that he was in a comfortable room, surrounded by people who loved him dearly. And sometimes he would remember that the comfortable room was his bedroom and that the people who loved him were his family . . . and sometimes he didn't.

I don't know if he remembered his baptism, but I find it comforting that, even when my son had forgotten his parents, he still remembered to turn to God in times of trouble. And while memory loss might seem like a cruel fate for anyone, especially a child, it was also a mercy since it erased so much of the pain he'd suffered as well. And it also served as a reminder to all of us that God's plan may be unknowable and God's reasons may be unknowable, but we should have faith that there is a plan and, despite what we suffer as that plan is revealed, that plan is good.

Chapter 12
Acceptance

Back on March 18, Jon and I took the boys to the Shedd Aquarium; the management had arranged a special behind-the-scenes tour. Jonny and Jacky fed stingrays and did some tricks with a walrus and a sea lion named Luna. She reminded us of our dog, Lucy, as she always looked for approval after finishing a trick. They also spent a lot of time speaking with trainers, and the whole tour lasted three hours. Both boys had a wonderful time, but shortly after we'd left the aquarium, Jonny became sad.

When I asked Jonny what was wrong, he told me he didn't think he was going to be OK. Apparently, several of the children at his school had told him he was going to die, and he was finally beginning to realize that his cancer might not be a passing thing. I wasn't sure what to say to a seven-year-old boy contemplating his own death; bear in mind that, at this point, neither Jon nor I had yet to accept this possibility ourselves. We tried to reassure Jonny his cancer was part of God's plan, that there were so many people praying for him and that his story was inspiring others who were going through similar troubles. His answer was simply, "How can I help others when I can't help myself?" Eventually he grew so upset that he threw up.

These were questions that Jon and I weren't prepared to answer. Parents never feel comfortable speaking with their children about death, even in an abstract sense. But when death isn't something far off that will happen decades in the future, when it's not just something that happens to elderly relatives or people on television, it becomes especially difficult. It comes down to two questions. The first question is, "Why am I dying?" and the answer is, "It's part of God's plan." The second question is, "Why is this part of God's plan?" and the answer is, "I don't know, but God loves you and that's what is most important." None of us know.

For the next six months, we continued the radiation treatments and chemotherapy, the various drug cocktails and tubes running in and out of Jonny's body. For the next six months, Jonny and I continued to draw support and comfort from the thousands of people following his struggle on Facebook.

We'd been told from the beginning that, if the cancer returned after the chemotherapy, the doctors could do nothing more for him. After all the treatments, medicines, and prayers, if the cancer came back, then it would kill my son. What a troubling thought that was, but one that made us trust in God's plan over and over again, day after day.

In the middle of October, the doctors confirmed that the cancer had returned. It was just one month after he finished his last round of chemotherapy, which we had all celebrated with glee and a party with family. Jonny was proud to ring that chemotherapy bell that indicated that he had finished his treatment.

Of course, we hadn't lost hope at that point. Our son was still alive and we always had hope. But at that point, we began to change the focus of our days with Jonny. God had the ability to heal Jonny, either on earth or in heaven. He was weaker and more disoriented than he'd been in earlier months. He no longer attended baseball games or took trips to the aquarium or big fund-raising/awareness-raising events. Our oncologist told us to take him home and to go on several trips before he died, but Jonny was too weak and his memory was gone. He longed to stay home to enjoy his family and dog. Now we were focused on making our son as comfortable as possible. Anyone who's ever had to place an elderly relative in hospice care will understand this shift in priorities, but we had to make this shift for an eight-year-old boy.

Because of Jonny's memory loss, all we had to do was make his present a comfortable one. We didn't have to worry about him remembering the pain he'd suffered in the past. And he was usually so tired he didn't dwell too much on the future. For Jonny, the only moment was the present, and that present moment was Jonny surrounded by people who loved and cared for him.

Jonny was our son, but his life didn't belong to Jon or me. His life belonged to God. We got to borrow him for eight beautiful years. This journey was not one that Jon or I would have chosen for him. If we could, we would have gladly preferred to take that journey ourselves instead. But it wasn't our choice who got cancer, it wasn't our choice who would take that journey, and ultimately it wasn't our choice how that journey ended. It was God and God alone. He doesn't work for us; we work for him.

Jonny's loss of memory helped him make peace with his cancer. For Jon and I, accepting God's plan was what we had to do to make peace with it. Another story I've found comforting concerns a caterpillar turning into a butterfly, which we shared often with Jonny.

Many times when Jonny would wonder "why me?" we would fake an answer. Truthfully, we wondered the same question. He wondered why he had to go through this, why

"Send me butterflies"

he had to be different than his friends, why he had to lose his hair and his hearing, why so much pain and suffering? We didn't know. But I told him that just when the caterpillar thought all was lost, it became a beautiful butterfly. The caterpillar doesn't know how to morph into a butterfly, and it doesn't know why. It just does. It becomes something more beautiful and capable than it ever could have imagined in its previous circumstances. Jonny was doing the same thing as that caterpillar.

Chapter 13
Two Balloons for Heaven

Nothing can ever fully prepare you for the death of a child, but by the beginning of December, it had been made clear to us that this most likely would happen. We had to discuss plans for hospice care with Jonny's doctors and decided our son would be better off at home with his family. Jon and I purchased a hospital bed and placed it in our bedroom so our son would never be alone, not one waking moment. I would lie next to him and hold his hand, talk to him, place our foreheads together, and stare into his eyes. We often had a routine of speaking about how much we loved each other. You see, Jonny and I shared a special love. He was my mini me, and we could tell how each other was feeling or going to say before the other one said it. We often had this exchange of words:

I would say, "I love you."

Jonny would respond, " I love you more."

I would reply, "Impossible."

Jonny would go on to say, "I love you more than the moon and the sky."

I would respond, "I love you to infinity."

He would chuckle and say, "OK, Momma, you got me there!"

Two weeks before Jonny passed, we were lying together, watching television. Jonny looked up at me and said, "I'm ready to die, Momma."

Caught off guard, I responded, "But Jonny, I wouldn't know what to do without you! I would be so lonely!"

He calmly said, "Momma, when you're lonely, talk to God."

I said, "Jonny, I would want to go with you."

He replied, "You have to stay here and take care of Jacky." Oh how my heart hurt. Jonny knew he was dying but needed to tell me to talk to God and take care of Jacky.

I spoke with several hospice workers about what we could expect near the end. They explained what usually happened during the last stages of brain cancer. After that, we had to make burial plans for my son. After everything we'd gone through over the past eleven months, we were now being told that nothing more could be done and that Jonny didn't have a lot of time left.

Since we were told that Jonny's remaining time could be measured in days, perhaps even hours, we decided to have

"Send me butterflies"

Christmas early. On December 12, Jacky and Jonny went to school together for the last time—Jacky pushing Jonny in his wheelchair—where the two of them joined their classmates standing along the hallway in a line singing Christmas carols while I stayed in the background and cried, trying to catch my breath, knowing this was going to be my son's last Christmas.

When we got back home, Jonny and Jacky received another surprise as Santa Claus and ten elves showed up with presents. Since Jon and I weren't involved in the gift buying that year, the entire family was surprised every time one of the boys unwrapped another present. Later that evening, my sister and niece arrived from Florida, and together we watched as a youth group gathered on our lawn to sing Christmas carols. Jonny was wrapped up in a chair with a heater and several blankets as he listened to the carols. He told me their voices were so good that they were singing him to sleep. Despite everything we'd suffered, Jacky told me it was the best Christmas ever. I have to agree, and I am so grateful to everyone who helped make it possible.

After our early Christmas, Jonny's condition deteriorated rapidly. You might think that something that slowly ate away at your body and made you weaker every day would at least end with a peaceful death, letting you quietly fade away. But in fact, Jonny had one of his most violent seizures on

December 13, after we'd put him on his drip, along with a catheter, leading us to the decision that he would need to be given a permanent IV drip of morphine. Probably the worst part of the whole attack came after it was over and Jonny said to me, "I can't live like Jacky." Seeing your child in pain is terrible, but not being able to say or do anything to make that pain stop is so much worse. Jonny would never have a life like his brother's and he knew it.

Jonny had been aware for some time that he might not survive his struggle with cancer. But by December, that had gone from a possibility to a near certainty, and we were all concerned about how he would handle it. How would you handle it? Even after living a full life, many people find they can't cope with the concept of dying. But at eight years old, Jonny already had a spiritual strength that so many of us lack. He would hold on to his cross, and when I asked if he was scared or worried, he would answer, "No. I feel safe with my cross. God is right here and the angels are all up there." When he spoke about the angels, he would wave above his head; while when he spoke about God, he would indicate a place beside his bed. He told me that he could hear the angels singing, and I often wished I could hear them as well, taking comfort in their presence. But they were there to comfort my son and not me.

"Send me butterflies"

And I've wondered if maybe Jonny's connection with God wasn't something that he learned from us. Maybe our relationship with God isn't something that we develop over years but something that we're born with, something that we slowly lose over time as we grow older and fill our lives with other "important" concerns that distract us from that relationship. Maybe we all feel God's presence when we're Jonny's age but forget over time. Maybe it takes an eight-year-old boy dying from cancer to remind us that God is with us every day, even when we don't notice Him. Maybe that's why pediatric cancer is part of God's plan.

As Jonny slipped in and out of consciousness as his life came to an end, I would snuggle with him and whisper, "Send me butterflies, send me butterflies so I know you are with me." A couple days before Jonny passed, he looked at Jon and me standing next to his bedside. He said, "I think I know how this is going to end, but I want to be with my family. I don't want to miss you!" He immediately put his arms around my neck and pulled me into his chest as if someone was trying to hang on or ground themselves. Jonny was so strong that I couldn't lift myself up.

I sobbed and said, "Honey, it's going to be OK. Everything is going to be OK." I said this because, in my eyes, everything was going to be OK—OK for Jonny, that is. Jonny never opened his eyes or spoke again after that day. I believe that is when Jesus and the angels came and took him to heaven. His little frail body was all that remained.

Jonny died on Christmas Eve, December 24, almost a year to the day he was first diagnosed with cancer. Jonny laid in my arms and took his last breath. It was the most horrific moment of my life.

Before he'd ever been diagnosed, Jonny had wanted to release a balloon on Christmas morning as a happy birthday message to Jesus. That Christmas had found us in an emergency room, dealing with what we had thought were simply bad migraine headaches, and we'd completely forgotten about the balloon. But the following year, before we had even buried Jonny, we thought about it again. I sometimes tell people that Jonny decided to wish Jesus a happy birthday in person that year. But those of us left behind decided to extend our birthday wishes to Jesus as well by finally releasing that balloon on Christmas morning, not only to celebrate His birth, but also to thank Him for all of our blessings.

Jonny was a blessing in my life, whether he lived to be eight or eighty. Every day I spent with him was a blessing, even the days when he was wracked by seizures, suffering from radiation treatment burns, vomiting every bite of food he ate, or asking me questions I couldn't answer about why

"Send me butterflies"

he had to suffer so much. Even the days when Jonny couldn't remember my name were blessings. And since Jonny was no longer with us, we decided to send up a second balloon for him as well, to let Jonny know we missed him, we loved him, and we were so grateful for all the joy and love he'd brought into our lives.

Jonny would go on to be a blessing in others' lives as well. During Jonny's treatment, we had many conversations regarding the lack of funding and awareness. We were all disappointed in the little 4% that is allocated for pediatric cancer from the National Cancer Institute. Jonny often would say during out conversations, "Momma, I just want what's fair. Fair is fair. I want 50–50!" He couldn't grasp how little his life mattered to those in the world, and neither could I.

A couple of months prior to Jonny's passing, we spoke to him about creating a foundation. He felt it was a good idea because he didn't "want any other kid to have cancer." We knew it would be a lot of work but also knew it would be important work. Shortly thereafter, we created the Kids Shouldn't Have Cancer Foundation in Memory of Jonny Wade. We used Jonny's own words to come up with the name.

Chapter 14
State of the Union

Among the many people who came to visit with Jonny was Illinois Congressman Rodney Davis. I'm not sure what Congressman Davis expected, but when he spoke with Jonny, he was surprised to find a boy who was both focused and surprisingly mature. They spoke about baseball for ten minutes before the congressman asked, "So, is there anything you want, Jonny?"

Jonny immediately pointed to his head and said, "I want help with this. I want more than four percent."

No doubt, Congressman Davis expected Jonny to ask for a toy or something easily fulfilled, but instead my eight-year-old son pressed the congressman about increasing NCI (National Cancer Institute) funding for pediatric cancer research. At the time, the NCI only allotted 3.8% of its budget to all pediatric cancer research. Jonny thought that an allotment should be 50 percent, since that was only fair. He said, "If they want me to be a man, they have to help me be a man!" Frankly, I can't think of a simpler or more effective way to state the case for increased funding. Congressman Davis was similarly impressed and promised to argue for that increased funding, inviting us to join him in Washington, DC. Jonny happily agreed to speak to Congressman Davis's colleagues.

I'm sure it's easy to make all sorts of promises to a child fighting cancer when you're in the same room with him, just as it's easy to make excuses later on for not following through with those promises. But Congressman Davis was true to his word and, on November 18, addressed the House of Representatives about increasing the funding allotment for pediatric cancer research, specifically citing Jonny's struggle. It was a moving presentation (do a quick search online and you should be available to find a video of it) that met with a great deal of support from other members of Congress. Unfortunately, due to Jonny's deteriorating health at that point—right around the time we were told his cancer had returned—we were unable to attend the event in person, but Congressman Davis has my gratitude for everything he's done to help both my son and every other child struggling with cancer.

After speaking to the congressman from our home, Jonny had said, "Me having cancer is worth it if I can help other kids." It's that selfless drive to help others that inspired Congressman Davis, and it's that same drive that inspires me

"Send me butterflies"

to continue this struggle. Because Jonny's story doesn't end with his passing. How could it with so many people left who still love him so much?

As it turned out, the next step in our journey occurred less than a month after Jonny's passing. On January 12, 2016, President Barack Obama gave his last State of the Union Address. As with every State of the Union Address, he covered a wide range of issues, but this year one issue in particular touched us personally. He spoke about cancer research in general terms, then surprised everyone listening with a bold statement; he launched an initiative that wasn't meant to merely increase funding or raise awareness of cancer, but rather to outright cure it. Dubbing it a Moonshot Initiative, he then asked Vice President Joe Biden to lead it. The vice president, who was sitting directly behind the president at the time, immediately accepted the responsibility.

Vice President Biden was a natural choice to lead this initiative. Besides the respect he's earned from both politicians and the general public, he's also been touched on a personal level by cancer. Seven months before the president's address, Joe Biden lost his son, Beau Biden, to brain cancer on May 30th.

Like most of the people who listened to the State of the Union Address, my family and I were surprised by the president's ambitious initiative. The nickname was inspired by President John F. Kennedy's "Moonshot" speech delivered over fifty years ago, in which he proposed the then-seemingly-impossible task of placing an American on the moon by the end of the 1960s. At the time, it no doubt seemed as ambitious as finding a cure for cancer within a decade must seem today.

However, unlike most of the people who listened to the State of Union Address, Jon, Jacky, and I were actually in attendance. We'd been invited to attend before Jonny had passed away, but we had no idea that the president would be making any statement in regard to cancer research. Even if we had known, we would have expected little more than promises of increased funding for pediatric cancer research. Instead we were told about something far more significant. If you saw the speech on television, you no doubt saw the standing ovation from those assembled; I was the first one to jump out of my seat. It was one of those unexpected moments that bring me a smile or enjoyment; I feel them once in a while and call them my "Jonny winks."

Afterward, Jacky got to meet with President Obama. Being eight years old, I'm sure he had no idea how big of a deal it was to meet the President of the United States. He was pleasant and joked that my Jacky was so handsome that maybe he'd be the next president. He then asked why he was

"Send me butterflies"

attending the State of the Union. Jacky replied, "My twin brother, Jonny, had brain cancer and died." Congressman Davis then informed the president of more of the details.

Afterward, when Jon and I met back up with Jacky since we were in the gallery above and Jacky was down on the floor, Congressman Rodney Davis said, "Jacky, tell your Mom and Dad who you met."

Jacky said, "The president."

Of course, I thought he was kidding and chuckled, saying, "You did not." Then Congressman Davis gave Jacky his phone with a picture of Jacky and President Obama. I was shocked but quickly said in my excited tone, "What? You did? Oh my gosh! What did you think of him?"

Jacky replied with a grin on his face, "He has soft hands."

It turned out that attending the State of the Union Address wasn't the end of our involvement with the president's challenge for the next decade. I met with the deputy director for Vice President Biden several months later. The Moonshot Initiative was going to be far more than just political showmanship. It's a serious project that will continue until the goal of a cancer cure is achieved. And I am honored to say that I was asked to be a pediatric cancer advocate for the cancer Moonshot Initiative.

Kimberly Denise Wade

    I have no idea how much influence Congressman Davis's speech on November 18 had on the president's decision to create a cancer cure initiative. I know that the call for increased funding for pediatric cancer received a great deal of support, and it's easy to imagine that a cancer cure initiative would receive a great deal of support as well. I do know that the congressman's meeting with Jonny was moving enough to motivate him to make that speech, and the fact that my family was invited to attend the State of the Union Address meant that we were still in his thoughts even after that November speech was made. In fact, he'd urged many of his fellow legislators to wear Team Jonny bracelets during the speech to show their support for increased funding for pediatric cancer research. And by "many," I mean approximately two hundred and fifty of them, many of whom took selfies with their wristbands and posted them to Twitter. Clearly, Jonny's words to Congressman Davis had motivated him more than I'd even hoped. I'm also certain that the congressman's actions motivated the president, at least in part, to announce a cancer cure initiative. I like to think that my son played some part in making this initiative a reality, and I look forward to being an active part in this wonderful project.

Chapter 15
Having Faith

One of the hardest things about maintaining faith is that you rarely get any clear answers to your questions. I believe Jonny's cancer was a part of God's plan. I believe Jonny's death was a part of God's plan. And I've accepted God's plan. But what is God's plan? What have I accepted for myself, my son, and the rest of my family?

Was it just an inspiration for Congressman Rodney Davis to push to increase funding for pediatric cancer research? Is that why my son suffered for a year? Was it so Congressman Davis's speech could, in some small way, influence the president to create his Moonshot Initiative? I can't know, but I don't believe that was all my son's suffering was meant to accomplish. His suffering was not meaningless.

I've mentioned all of the support I've received from Facebook followers and various celebrities. I've mentioned the fund-raisers that helped us pay for all of Jonny's medication and tests. I've mentioned the doctors, nurses, and other caregivers who helped Jonny and my family through this difficult time.

And I've always thought of them as being there to help us, as God's way of making our burden easier.

But what if all those people, all those thousands of people who got to know Jonny, either in person or through my numerous postings about him, were being helped as well? What if their lives were also changed by this amazing eight-year-old boy who maintained his faith and selflessness until the final day of his life? What if your life is changed, even in some small way, by reading this book about Jonny's last year on earth?

Of course, you'd probably heard of pediatric cancer before you started reading this book. More than likely, you've seen some of those television commercials from organizations that raise money for cancer research and you've seen some of the cancer survivors: smiling bald children with discreet little IV lines running in their arms or slim feeding tubes running up their noses. They always look so happy in those commercials, and Jonny had his share of happy days during his last year.

But pediatric cancer is more of the suffering, the vomiting every single day, and losing weight because you can't keep any food down. Pediatric cancer is a child crying because he's in pain all the time. Pediatric cancer is a child growing weaker and weaker as the seizures grow stronger and stronger.

"Send me butterflies"

Pediatric cancer is losing your sight, your hearing, the use of your arms and legs, control of your bodily functions, and even your memory. Pediatric cancer is treatments that leave you burned, delirious, and permanently disabled. Pediatric cancer is a mother watching all of that happen to the person she loves most in the entire world and not being able to do a thing to stop it. Maybe they'd get more money if they showed all of that in a commercial.

Maybe commercials don't show the ugly realities of pediatric cancer because the organizations fear people would tune out and not support them. Maybe they believe people don't want to dwell on all of that depressing stuff. But I'd been writing about the ugly side of pediatric cancer for a year and got increased support from a growing number of people every day. I've said before that, if you've followed my Facebook posts about Jonny, then you know Jonny and you know me. Well, if you've followed my Facebook posts, you probably have a much better idea about the realities of pediatric cancer, at least better than what you see in commercials. And maybe that was God's plan: to show people what it's like, what it's really like, to go through pediatric cancer; not just the bald, smiling faces.

I truly believe God's plan for my son didn't end with his death. Whatever good Jonny's suffering was meant to accomplish hasn't finished. And that means that I now have to focus on something besides God's plan for my son. I have to think about God's plan for me.

I've already mentioned the State of the Union Address and my own involvement in the Moonshot Initiative. I'm not a doctor. I'm not a researcher. Sure, I know a lot more about cancer treatment than I did two years ago, but there's no way I'll ever be able to find a cure for cancer. And that's not the part I've been asked to play in this struggle. Because what I can do instead is increase awareness about the realities of pediatric cancer and raise funds for those who are doctors and researchers that specialize in pediatric cancers. For over a year now, I've been telling Jonny's story, Jacky's story, Jon's story, and my story. And those stories—the story of Team Jonny—are being heard by an ever-growing number of people. So maybe God's plan for me is to continue telling that story to as many people as possible to gain support.

I can do that. God gave me the talent of communication and connecting with people.

As for finding the people who need to hear this story, I didn't have to search for long. In fact, they found me and still do.

I was first approached to speak in public in early February of 2016. The organizers of a women's conference in Missouri

"Send me butterflies"

were familiar with my story and wanted me to share it with them. On February 21, I had my first public speaking engagement. Five hundred women attended, and while many people have a terrible fear of public speaking, I found that it came quite easy to me. I never felt nervous in front of them. After all, I'd already shared my story with thousands of people. In this case, I was able to see their faces as I spoke, which in some ways made it even easier. Since that first engagement, I've spoken with many other groups about the importance of increasing funding for pediatric cancer, maintaining faith through times of suffering, and learning how to nurture others who are suffering.

Jonny believed that the reason he got cancer was so he could help others. He never lost his faith nor his desire to help those around him. When people see the tagline of my presentation, "Broken Crayons Still Color," a lot of them assume that Jonny is the broken crayon. But he never broke, not through all of his suffering.

The broken crayons are Jon, Jacky, and all the other people who are left behind after losing someone to cancer or who have had their own type of suffering in their lives. The broken crayon I've been talking about all this time is me. But whatever plan God has for me, it isn't finished yet. It's a popular belief that God never hands us more burdens than we can bear, but I believe that God, in fact, does hand us far more than we can bear. He heaps these burdens on us so we learn to turn to one another for help and to lean on Him. And if those burdens sometimes break us, then even that is part of God's plan. Broken crayons still color, and broken souls can still love, grow, and reach out to one another.

So, the next time you feel broken, remember, you can go on to color more rainbows for others. I hope my story helps you discover and accept God's plan for you.

About the Author

Kimberly Denise Wade is a motivational speaker who inspires audiences with the story of her son Jonny, who bravely fought pediatric cancer. Kimberly currently is president of the Kids Shouldn't Have Cancer Foundation in Memory of JonnyWade. She also serves as a pediatric cancer advocate for Vice President Joe Biden's Cancer Moonshot initiative, a national effort dedicated to doubling the rate of progress toward finding a cure for cancer. She lives with her husband, Jon, and Jonny's twin brother, Jackson (nicknamed "Jacky"), in Jerseyville, Illinois, where they attend First Baptist Church.

KimberlyDeniseWade.com

Made in the USA
San Bernardino, CA
20 November 2016